The Power of Compassion: Exploring Social Welfare Policy for Students

Stefania Rossi

Copyright © [2023]

Title: The Power of Compassion: Exploring Social Welfare Policy for Students

Author's: Stefania Rossi.

This book was printed and published by [Publisher's: Stefania Rossi] in [2023]

ISBN:

TABLE OF CONTENTS

Chapter 1: Introduction to Social Welfare Policy

Understanding Social Welfare Policy

Social welfare policy plays a crucial role in addressing the needs of individuals and communities in society. It encompasses a broad range of programs, initiatives, and legislation aimed at promoting the well-being and social justice of all citizens. As students entering the field of public policy, it is essential to grasp the fundamental concepts and principles that underpin social welfare policy.

This subchapter titled "Understanding Social Welfare Policy" aims to provide students with a comprehensive overview of the multifaceted nature of social welfare policy and its significance in shaping society. By delving into the various aspects of this topic, students will gain a deeper understanding of the complex issues involved and the impact of policy decisions on individuals and communities.

The chapter begins by defining social welfare policy and its objectives. It explores the historical context of social welfare policy, tracing its roots back to the Progressive Era and the New Deal in the United States. Understanding the historical development of social welfare policy is crucial to comprehend its evolution and the underlying ideologies that have shaped its current form.

Next, the chapter examines the key components and principles of social welfare policy. Students will learn about the different types of social welfare programs, including income support, healthcare, education, and housing. They will also explore the principles of equity, social justice, and human rights that guide the formulation and implementation of social welfare policies.

The subchapter further explores the role of various stakeholders in social welfare policy, including government agencies, nonprofit organizations, and advocacy groups. Students will gain insights into the challenges and opportunities faced by these stakeholders in influencing policy decisions and addressing the needs of vulnerable populations effectively.

Moreover, the chapter discusses the impact of social welfare policy on different demographic groups, such as children, the elderly, individuals with disabilities, and minority populations. By examining the intersectionality of social welfare policy, students will gain a deeper understanding of how policies can either perpetuate or alleviate social inequalities.

To enhance students' understanding, the subchapter includes real-world case studies and examples that illustrate the practical application of social welfare policy. These case studies shed light on the successes and failures of past policies, allowing students to critically analyze their implications and draw valuable lessons for future policy development.

In conclusion, "Understanding Social Welfare Policy" is a vital subchapter in the book "The Power of Compassion: Exploring Social Welfare Policy for Students." It equips students with the knowledge and analytical skills necessary to navigate the intricacies of social welfare policy and empowers them to contribute meaningfully to the field of public policy. By comprehending the complexities and implications of social welfare policy, students can become agents of change in building a more equitable and compassionate society.

Importance of Social Welfare Policy for Students

Title: Importance of Social Welfare Policy for Students

Introduction:

Welcome to "The Power of Compassion: Exploring Social Welfare Policy for Students." In this subchapter, we will delve into the significance of social welfare policy specifically for students. As young individuals studying in various fields, it is crucial for students to understand the impact of social welfare policies on their lives and the broader public policy landscape.

1. Enhancing Accessibility to Education: Social welfare policies play a vital role in ensuring equal access to education for all students. These policies aim to eliminate financial barriers and provide resources such as scholarships, grants, and student loans. By promoting educational opportunities, social welfare policies empower students from diverse backgrounds to pursue their academic goals and contribute to society.

2. Addressing Basic Needs: For students facing financial hardship, social welfare policies provide essential support to meet their basic needs. Programs like food assistance, housing subsidies, and healthcare benefits ensure that students can focus on their studies without the burden of hunger or inadequate living conditions. By alleviating these concerns, social welfare policies create a conducive environment for academic success.

3. Promoting Mental Health and Well-being: Social welfare policies also encompass mental health services, which are crucial for students' overall well-being. Recognizing the challenges

faced by students, policies may include counseling services, mental health awareness campaigns, and affordable access to therapy. By prioritizing mental health, social welfare policies support students in managing stress, anxiety, and other mental health issues, ultimately enhancing their academic performance.

4.   Fostering   Diversity   and   Inclusion: Social welfare policies promote diversity and inclusion by ensuring equal opportunities for students from marginalized groups. These policies counteract discrimination and provide resources for underrepresented students, fostering a more equitable educational environment. By valuing diversity, social welfare policies enrich the student experience and prepare them to contribute to a diverse society.

Conclusion:
In conclusion, understanding the importance of social welfare policies for students is essential for navigating the challenges of higher education. By promoting accessibility to education, addressing basic needs, supporting mental health, and fostering diversity and inclusion, these policies create an environment where students can thrive academically and personally. As students pursuing public policy, it is crucial to engage with social welfare policies, advocate for necessary reforms, and contribute to an inclusive society that values the well-being and success of all students.

Chapter 2: Historical Overview of Social Welfare Policy

Origins of Social Welfare Policy

Social welfare policy is a crucial aspect of public policy that aims to address the needs and well-being of individuals, families, and communities. To understand the current state of social welfare policy, it is essential to explore its origins and how it has evolved over time.

The roots of social welfare policy can be traced back to ancient civilizations, where communities established systems to provide assistance to the vulnerable members. In ancient Rome, for example, the concept of public assistance emerged, with laws enacted to support the poor, disabled, and elderly. Similarly, in ancient China, the idea of social welfare was ingrained in Confucian philosophy, emphasizing the importance of collective responsibility and care for the less fortunate.

During the Middle Ages, religious institutions played a significant role in providing social welfare. Churches and monasteries became centers of charity, offering food, shelter, and healthcare to those in need. With the rise of Protestantism, the notion of individual responsibility gained prominence, leading to the establishment of workhouses and poor laws in Europe.

The industrial revolution marked a turning point in social welfare policy. The rapid urbanization and harsh working conditions of the 19th century led to growing social inequality and heightened awareness of the need for intervention. Reformers like Charles

Dickens and Jacob Riis shed light on the plight of the poor, sparking public outrage and demanding change.

In response, governments began to implement social welfare policies to alleviate poverty and address social ills. The British Poor Law Amendment Act of 1834, for instance, introduced workhouses and outdoor relief, while the German Chancellor Otto von Bismarck pioneered the concept of social insurance, establishing the first modern welfare state.

The Great Depression of the 1930s marked another significant shift in social welfare policy. The economic crisis exposed the inadequacy of existing measures, leading to the development of comprehensive social programs in the United States, such as Social Security and the New Deal.

In recent decades, social welfare policy has continued to evolve in response to changing societal needs and values. Issues such as income inequality, healthcare access, and environmental sustainability have gained prominence, shaping the policy agenda.

Understanding the origins of social welfare policy provides a foundation for students studying public policy. It highlights the historical context and the societal forces that have shaped the development of social welfare programs. By examining the past, students can gain insights into the challenges and opportunities that lay ahead, equipping them with the knowledge and tools to advocate for effective and compassionate social welfare policies in the future.

Evolution of Social Welfare Policy in Different Countries

Introduction:

Understanding the evolution of social welfare policies is crucial for students studying public policy. The development of social welfare policies in various countries has been influenced by a multitude of factors, including political, economic, and social conditions. This subchapter aims to provide students with an overview of the evolution of social welfare policies in different countries, allowing them to gain a comprehensive understanding of how these policies have developed and adapted over time.

Historical Context:

To comprehend the evolution of social welfare policies, it is essential to examine the historical context of each country. Factors such as colonialism, industrialization, and political ideologies have significantly shaped the development of these policies. For instance, in European countries, the emergence of welfare states after World War II was a response to the devastation caused by the conflict, while in some Asian countries, social welfare policies were influenced by their post-colonial struggles for independence.

Policy Approaches:

Different countries have adopted varying approaches to social welfare policies. Students will explore the differences between welfare models such as the liberal, conservative, and social democratic models, which have shaped policies in countries like the United States, United Kingdom, and Sweden, respectively. By comparing these approaches, students can understand how political ideologies and social values influence the design and implementation of social welfare policies.

Impact and Effectiveness:

Analyzing the impact and effectiveness of social welfare policies is another crucial aspect for students studying public policy. This subchapter will delve into case studies from countries like the United States, Canada, and Germany, highlighting the successes and challenges faced by their social welfare systems. Students will gain insights into how these policies have affected poverty rates, healthcare access, education, and social mobility.

Current Challenges:

Lastly, the subchapter will address the current challenges faced by social welfare policies in different countries. Globalization, demographic changes, and economic recessions have presented new obstacles and opportunities for policymakers. Students will explore innovative approaches and policy reforms that aim to address these challenges, such as universal basic income, healthcare reforms, and supporting vulnerable populations.

Conclusion:

Understanding the evolution of social welfare policies in different countries is essential for students studying public policy. By examining historical contexts, policy approaches, impact and effectiveness, and current challenges, students can gain a comprehensive understanding of how these policies have developed and adapted over time. This knowledge will equip students to analyze and contribute to the ongoing debates and reforms in social welfare policies, fostering their ability to shape a more compassionate and equitable society.

Impact of Historical Events on Social Welfare Policy

Introduction:
In the realm of public policy, understanding the historical context and events that shaped social welfare policies is crucial for students aspiring to make a difference in society. This subchapter delves into the impact of historical events on social welfare policy, unraveling the interconnectedness between past events and the policies that emerged as a response to societal needs. By exploring historical events, students gain insight into the evolution of social welfare policies and the factors that influenced their development.

The   Great   Depression:
The Great Depression of the 1930s serves as a pivotal event that significantly influenced social welfare policies. As the economic crisis deepened, millions of Americans faced unemployment, poverty, and homelessness. In response, the government implemented the New Deal, which introduced several social welfare programs such as Social Security and unemployment insurance. Students studying public policy can analyze the New Deal's impact on poverty alleviation and the development of a safety net for vulnerable populations.

The   Civil   Rights   Movement:
The Civil Rights Movement of the 1950s and 1960s brought attention to racial inequality and discrimination in the United States. This movement had a profound impact on social welfare policies, prompting the passing of landmark legislation such as the Civil Rights Act of 1964 and the Voting Rights Act of 1965. Students can examine how these policies aimed to eliminate racial discrimination and create

equal opportunities in areas such as education, employment, and housing.

The   Feminist   Movement:
The feminist movement, which gained momentum in the 1960s and 1970s, challenged gender inequalities and influenced social welfare policies. The fight for women's rights led to legislation such as the Equal Pay Act of 1963 and the Title IX of the Education Amendments of 1972. These policies aimed to address gender disparities in employment and education, empowering women and promoting gender equality.

The   Great   Recession:
The Great Recession of 2008 had a profound impact on the social welfare landscape. As unemployment rates soared and families faced foreclosure, the government responded with measures such as the American Recovery and Reinvestment Act of 2009, which aimed to stimulate the economy and provide assistance to those affected. Students can explore the effectiveness of these policies in mitigating the impact of the recession and preventing long-term economic and social consequences.

Conclusion:
Studying the impact of historical events on social welfare policy allows students to understand how society has responded to crises and challenges throughout history. By examining the policies that emerged from these events, students gain insight into the complexities of public policy and the importance of addressing societal needs. This knowledge equips students in the field of public policy to advocate for

change, create effective policies, and contribute to the betterment of society.

Chapter 3: Key Concepts in Social Welfare Policy

Social Justice and Equality

In today's society, social justice and equality are two concepts that have gained significant attention and importance. These ideas form the backbone of any progressive society, and as students interested in public policy, it is crucial for us to understand their significance and implications. This subchapter will delve into the core aspects of social justice and equality, exploring their definitions, historical contexts, and their role in shaping social welfare policies.

Social justice can be defined as the fair and equitable distribution of resources, opportunities, and privileges within a society. It encompasses notions of fairness, impartiality, and the pursuit of equal rights for all individuals, regardless of their background or circumstances. Equality, on the other hand, refers to the state of being equal, where all individuals have equal access to resources, opportunities, and rights.

Throughout history, marginalized groups have faced discrimination, injustice, and inequality in various forms. From racial discrimination and gender inequality to economic disparities and social exclusion, these issues have persisted and continue to hinder the progress of societies worldwide. Consequently, social welfare policies have emerged as a means to address these inequalities and strive for a more just and equal society.

Understanding the complexities of social justice and equality is crucial for students interested in public policy. By studying the historical context and analyzing the root causes of these issues, we can gain valuable insights into the development and implementation of effective social welfare policies. This subchapter will explore various theories and frameworks that guide policymaking in the pursuit of social justice and equality.

Additionally, we will examine case studies and real-life examples that highlight the impacts of social welfare policies on marginalized communities. By analyzing these examples, we can assess the successes, challenges, and potential areas for improvement in addressing social justice and equality through policy interventions.

Ultimately, this subchapter aims to equip students with the knowledge and tools necessary to contribute to the advancement of social justice and equality through public policy. By understanding the concepts, historical context, and practical implications of these ideas, we can become effective advocates for change and work towards building a more inclusive and equitable society.

In conclusion, social justice and equality are fundamental concepts that shape the development and implementation of social welfare policies. As students interested in public policy, it is crucial to understand their significance, historical context, and practical implications. Through this subchapter, we will explore the theories, frameworks, and real-life examples that guide policymaking in the pursuit of social justice and equality. By doing so, we can contribute to the creation of a fairer and more just society for all.

Poverty and Inequality

In our modern society, poverty and inequality are two interconnected and complex issues that demand our attention. As students interested in public policy, it is crucial to understand the causes and consequences of poverty and inequality, as well as the potential solutions that can be implemented to address these pressing challenges.

Poverty, defined as the lack of access to basic necessities such as food, shelter, and healthcare, is a pervasive issue that affects millions of individuals and families around the world. It is not only a matter of material deprivation but also a violation of human rights. Poverty can result from various factors, including limited educational opportunities, unemployment, discrimination, and inadequate social welfare policies.

Inequality, on the other hand, refers to the unequal distribution of wealth, income, and opportunities within a society. It manifests in different forms, such as economic inequality, educational inequality, and social inequality. Inequality not only perpetuates poverty but also undermines social cohesion, economic growth, and democracy. It is a challenge that must be addressed to ensure a just and equitable society for all.

Understanding the causes and consequences of poverty and inequality is only the first step. As students, we have the power to drive change and create a more compassionate society. By studying social welfare policies, we can identify effective strategies to combat poverty and reduce inequality.

One crucial approach is to develop comprehensive social safety nets that provide a basic level of support for all individuals, regardless of their socioeconomic status. This can include programs such as universal healthcare, affordable housing initiatives, and income support schemes. By ensuring that everyone has access to essential resources and services, we can alleviate poverty and reduce inequality.

Additionally, addressing the root causes of poverty and inequality requires systemic changes. This involves promoting equal opportunities through quality education, job training programs, and inclusive economic policies. By investing in human capital and empowering individuals, we can break the cycle of poverty and create a more equitable society.

Furthermore, it is important to acknowledge and challenge the structural barriers that contribute to inequality, such as discrimination based on race, gender, or ethnicity. Advocating for policies that promote social justice and equality can help dismantle these barriers and create a more inclusive society.

As students interested in public policy, we have the opportunity to shape the future and contribute to the development of compassionate social welfare policies. By understanding the complexities of poverty and inequality, and by advocating for effective solutions, we can work towards a society that values compassion, justice, and equal opportunity for all.

Human Rights and Social Welfare

In today's world, the interconnectedness of human rights and social welfare is undeniable. Human rights, as defined by the United Nations, are the basic rights and freedoms to which all individuals are entitled, regardless of their race, gender, religion, or social status. Social welfare, on the other hand, refers to the collective efforts of a society to provide for the well-being of its members, particularly those who are vulnerable or marginalized.

Understanding the intersection of human rights and social welfare is crucial for students interested in public policy. This subchapter aims to shed light on this important relationship, exploring how human rights principles inform and shape social welfare policies.

One key aspect of human rights and social welfare is the idea of social justice. Social justice is about ensuring that every individual has equal access to opportunities, resources, and benefits within society. It recognizes the inherent dignity and worth of every person, emphasizing the need to eliminate discrimination, inequality, and poverty.

The principles of human rights provide a framework for evaluating social welfare policies and programs. Human rights-based approaches to social welfare prioritize the empowerment of individuals, their participation in decision-making processes, and the recognition of their rights to education, healthcare, housing, and social security.

Students studying public policy can explore how human rights frameworks can guide the development and implementation of social welfare policies. By understanding the principles of nondiscrimination, equality, and participation, students can advocate for policies that address the needs of vulnerable populations and promote social inclusion.

Moreover, this subchapter examines the role of international human rights treaties and conventions in shaping social welfare policies at both national and global levels. Students will learn about the Universal Declaration of Human Rights and other key international instruments that provide a foundation for social welfare policies worldwide.

Additionally, the subchapter delves into specific areas where human rights and social welfare intersect, such as child welfare, healthcare, education, and the rights of persons with disabilities. Through case studies and examples, students will gain a deeper understanding of how social welfare policies can reinforce or undermine human rights principles.

Overall, this subchapter aims to equip students with the knowledge and tools to critically analyze and advocate for social welfare policies that uphold human rights. By understanding the inherent connection between human rights and social welfare, students can become effective agents of change, working towards a more just and equitable society for all.

Chapter 4: The Role of Government in Social Welfare Policy

Government's Responsibility in Ensuring Social Welfare

In today's complex and interconnected world, the government plays a crucial role in promoting and ensuring social welfare for its citizens. As students studying public policy, it is essential to understand the various ways in which the government fulfills its responsibility towards the well-being of society. This subchapter will explore the government's role in creating and implementing social welfare policies that address the needs of the population.

One of the primary responsibilities of the government is to provide access to essential services such as healthcare, education, and housing. By investing in these sectors, the government endeavors to guarantee that every individual has the opportunity to live a dignified life. For instance, public healthcare systems ensure that medical services are accessible and affordable to all, regardless of their socioeconomic background. Similarly, educational policies aim to bridge the gap between the privileged and the marginalized, offering equal opportunities for quality education.

Furthermore, the government is responsible for devising social safety nets to protect vulnerable populations. These safety nets include programs such as unemployment benefits, disability allowances, and welfare assistance for low-income families. By implementing these measures, the government aims to alleviate poverty and reduce inequality, ensuring that no one is left behind in times of economic hardship.

Another aspect of the government's responsibility lies in creating an inclusive society that respects and protects the rights of all individuals. This involves implementing policies that promote gender equality, racial justice, and LGBTQ+ rights. By addressing systemic inequalities and discrimination, the government fosters a society that embraces diversity and upholds social justice.

Moreover, the government plays a crucial role in disaster management and emergency response. During times of crisis, it is the government's responsibility to coordinate relief efforts, provide aid, and ensure the safety of its citizens. By investing in disaster preparedness and response mechanisms, the government can minimize the impact of natural disasters and protect the lives and livelihoods of its people.

In conclusion, the government holds a significant responsibility in ensuring social welfare. By investing in essential services, implementing social safety nets, promoting inclusivity, and managing crises effectively, the government plays a pivotal role in creating a just and compassionate society. As students of public policy, it is crucial for us to understand and critically analyze the government's role in social welfare, as well as advocate for policies that prioritize the well-being of all citizens. Together, we can work towards building a more equitable and compassionate society for generations to come.

Government Agencies and Programs for Social Welfare

In today's complex society, the government plays a crucial role in addressing social issues and ensuring the well-being of its citizens. This subchapter aims to introduce students to the various government agencies and programs dedicated to social welfare. By understanding these entities, students can gain insight into the development and implementation of public policies that aim to alleviate poverty, promote social justice, and improve the overall quality of life for individuals and communities.

One prominent government agency focused on social welfare is the Department of Health and Human Services (DHHS). This department oversees a vast array of programs and initiatives aimed at improving public health, human services, and social welfare. Within the DHHS, students will learn about agencies such as the Centers for Disease Control and Prevention (CDC), the Food and Drug Administration (FDA), and the Administration for Children and Families (ACF). These agencies work together to address critical issues such as healthcare access, child welfare, and public health emergencies.

Another essential government agency to explore is the Department of Housing and Urban Development (HUD). This agency is responsible for developing and implementing policies and programs that address housing needs and promote community development. Students will gain insight into initiatives such as public housing assistance, affordable housing programs, and community development block grants, which aim to create safe and affordable housing options for low-income individuals and families.

Additionally, the subchapter will delve into the role of the Social Security Administration (SSA) in providing social welfare benefits to eligible individuals. Students will learn about programs such as Social Security Disability Insurance (SSDI) and Supplemental Security Income (SSI), which offer financial assistance to individuals with disabilities, the elderly, and low-income individuals and families.

Furthermore, the subchapter will touch upon other government programs, including Temporary Assistance for Needy Families (TANF), the Women, Infants, and Children (WIC) program, and the National School Lunch Program (NSLP). These programs are designed to provide temporary financial assistance, nutritional support, and educational resources to vulnerable populations, particularly children and families living in poverty.

Through exploring these government agencies and programs, students will develop a comprehensive understanding of the critical role the government plays in promoting social welfare and improving the lives of its citizens. By analyzing the implementation and effectiveness of these entities, students will be better equipped to contribute to the field of public policy and advocate for evidence-based solutions to social issues.

Public-Private Partnerships in Social Welfare

In recent years, the concept of public-private partnerships (PPPs) has gained significant attention in the field of social welfare. This subchapter aims to explore the role of PPPs in addressing social welfare challenges and the potential benefits they offer.

Public-private partnerships refer to collaborative efforts between government agencies and private entities to deliver social welfare services and programs. These partnerships leverage the strengths and resources of both sectors to achieve mutually agreed-upon goals. Students studying public policy have a crucial role to play in understanding and promoting effective PPPs in social welfare.

One of the primary benefits of PPPs is increased efficiency and effectiveness in service delivery. By combining the expertise and resources of the public and private sectors, PPPs can often achieve better outcomes than traditional government programs alone. Private organizations bring innovation, flexibility, and specialized knowledge to the table, while the government provides regulatory oversight and access to public funds.

Moreover, PPPs also have the potential to address the limitations of public funding in social welfare. As government budgets face constraints, partnering with private entities allows for additional financial resources to be mobilized. This can lead to expanded service coverage, improved quality of services, and increased access for marginalized populations.

However, it is crucial for students to understand that PPPs are not without challenges. One key concern is the potential risk of privatization and the erosion of the public sector's role in social welfare. It is essential to strike a balance between leveraging private sector efficiencies and maintaining the government's responsibility for ensuring equitable access to services.

Additionally, accountability and transparency are crucial aspects of successful PPPs. Students need to explore mechanisms for monitoring and evaluating PPPs to ensure that public funds are used effectively and that the needs of vulnerable populations are adequately addressed.

Overall, public-private partnerships have the potential to transform social welfare policy and improve the lives of individuals and communities. Students studying public policy play a vital role in understanding the intricacies of PPPs and advocating for their responsible implementation. By harnessing the power of collaboration between the public and private sectors, we can create innovative solutions to pressing social challenges and build a more compassionate society.

Chapter 5: Social Welfare Policy and Education

Importance of Education in Social Welfare

Education plays a crucial role in fostering social welfare and is a fundamental aspect of public policy. In a rapidly changing world, acquiring knowledge and skills through education not only empowers individuals but also contributes to the overall well-being of society. This subchapter explores the significance of education in promoting social welfare, and its relevance to students interested in public policy.

Education is the key to self-improvement and personal growth. It equips individuals with the necessary tools to navigate through life, make informed decisions, and pursue their aspirations. By providing access to quality education, societies can break the cycle of poverty, inequality, and social exclusion. Education empowers individuals to overcome socio-economic barriers and enhances their opportunities for a better future.

Furthermore, education is a catalyst for social change. It fosters critical thinking, promotes empathy, and encourages active citizenship. Students who receive a well-rounded education are more likely to actively engage in their communities, advocate for social justice, and contribute to the development of inclusive policies. By equipping students with a deep understanding of social welfare issues, education empowers them to become agents of change and work towards creating a more equitable society.

Education also has a direct impact on public policy. Policies related to education shape the future of societies, impacting economic growth, social cohesion, and overall well-being. Students interested in public policy have a unique opportunity to contribute to the design and implementation of education policies that address the needs of diverse populations. By studying the intersection of education and social welfare, students can gain insights into the challenges faced by marginalized communities and propose innovative solutions to bridge gaps in access and quality.

Moreover, education is essential for building a skilled workforce that drives economic development. By investing in education, societies can improve productivity, stimulate innovation, and foster sustainable economic growth. Students who pursue education in fields related to public policy can contribute to shaping policies that promote economic opportunities, reduce unemployment, and address skills gaps.

In conclusion, education is of utmost importance in promoting social welfare, and its relevance to students interested in public policy cannot be overstated. By acquiring knowledge, skills, and perspectives through education, individuals can transform their own lives and contribute to the betterment of society. Through their understanding of the intersection between education and social welfare, students can become advocates for inclusive policies and work towards creating a more equitable society.

Access to Education for Underprivileged Students

Education is a fundamental human right that should be accessible to all individuals, regardless of their socioeconomic background. Unfortunately, many underprivileged students face significant barriers when it comes to accessing quality education. This subchapter aims to shed light on the challenges faced by these students and the importance of addressing the issue within the realm of public policy.

Underprivileged students often come from low-income families, where the financial burden of education can be overwhelming. Many cannot afford to attend schools that provide quality education, forcing them into underfunded and overcrowded institutions. This lack of resources directly affects the quality of education they receive, perpetuating a cycle of poverty and limiting their opportunities for a brighter future.

In addition to financial constraints, underprivileged students often lack the necessary support systems to thrive academically. They may come from disadvantaged neighborhoods with limited access to educational resources, such as libraries or tutoring centers. As a result, they struggle to keep up with their peers, leading to lower academic performance and limited opportunities for higher education.

Public policy plays a crucial role in addressing these disparities and ensuring equal access to education for all students. Governments should prioritize investments in education, allocating sufficient funds to improve the infrastructure and resources of schools in underprivileged areas. This includes providing modern technology, well-trained teachers, and access to extracurricular activities that enhance the learning experience.

Furthermore, public policy should focus on implementing targeted interventions to support underprivileged students. This can be achieved through scholarship programs, grants, and financial aid initiatives that reduce the financial burden on families. Additionally, after-school programs and mentorship opportunities can provide the necessary academic support and guidance to help underprivileged students succeed.

By addressing the issue of access to education for underprivileged students, public policy can create a more inclusive and equitable society. Providing equal opportunities for education not only benefits the individual students, but also has far-reaching societal impacts. It can break the cycle of poverty, reduce inequality, and contribute to economic growth by nurturing a skilled and educated workforce.

As students, we have the power to advocate for change. By raising awareness about the challenges faced by underprivileged students and supporting policies that promote equal access to education, we can contribute to creating a fairer society. Together, we can harness the power of compassion to ensure that every student, regardless of their background, has the opportunity to reach their full potential through education.

Educational Policies for Social Inclusion

Education is a fundamental right that should be accessible to all individuals, regardless of their background or social status. Unfortunately, in many societies, certain groups face barriers that prevent them from fully participating in the educational system. To address this issue, governments and policymakers have implemented educational policies for social inclusion, aiming to create a fair and equitable education system.

One of the key aspects of educational policies for social inclusion is the promotion of equal opportunities. These policies focus on ensuring that every student, regardless of their socioeconomic status, race, gender, or disability, has access to quality education. This includes providing scholarships, grants, and financial assistance to students from disadvantaged backgrounds, as well as creating inclusive learning environments that cater to the needs of diverse students.

In addition to equal opportunities, educational policies for social inclusion also emphasize the importance of diversity and cultural understanding in the classroom. By implementing multicultural education programs, schools can foster an inclusive environment where students can learn about different cultures, traditions, and perspectives. This not only helps to break down stereotypes and prejudices but also prepares students to thrive in a globalized world.

Furthermore, educational policies for social inclusion recognize the unique challenges faced by students with disabilities. These policies advocate for inclusive education, ensuring that students with disabilities are provided with necessary accommodations and support so they can fully participate in mainstream classrooms. This may include assistive technologies, specialized teaching methods, and individualized education plans tailored to their specific needs.

Moreover, educational policies for social inclusion also address the issue of educational inequality in rural and remote areas. These policies strive to bridge the gap by improving access to educational resources, such as libraries, internet connectivity, and extracurricular activities. By investing in the infrastructure and resources needed, governments can ensure that all students, regardless of their geographical location, have an equal opportunity to receive a quality education.

In conclusion, educational policies for social inclusion play a crucial role in creating a fair and equitable education system. These policies aim to provide equal opportunities, promote diversity and cultural understanding, support students with disabilities, and bridge the gap in educational inequality. By implementing these policies, governments and policymakers can ensure that all students have the chance to reach their full potential and contribute to society. As students, it is important to be aware of these policies and advocate for their implementation, as they are essential for creating a more inclusive and compassionate society.

Chapter 6: Health and Social Welfare Policy

Healthcare Access and Social Welfare

In today's society, access to healthcare is a fundamental aspect of social welfare that greatly impacts individuals and communities. Understanding the intersection between healthcare access and social welfare is crucial for students interested in public policy, as it provides insight into the challenges and opportunities for creating a more equitable and inclusive society.

Healthcare access refers to the ability of individuals to obtain the necessary medical services, treatments, and resources they need to maintain their physical and mental well-being. However, access to healthcare is not universal, and disparities exist based on factors such as income, race, ethnicity, and geographic location. These disparities have significant consequences for individuals who are unable to afford or access healthcare services, leading to poorer health outcomes and exacerbating existing social inequalities.

One of the key issues surrounding healthcare access is the affordability of healthcare services. Many individuals, particularly those from low-income backgrounds, struggle to afford health insurance premiums, deductibles, and co-pays. This financial burden often leads to delayed or forgone medical treatments, putting individuals at risk of further health complications. As students interested in public policy, it is essential to explore strategies that address these affordability challenges, such as expanding Medicaid, implementing subsidies, or advocating for universal healthcare.

Furthermore, healthcare access is not solely determined by financial barriers. Social determinants of health, such as education, employment, and housing, also play a significant role in determining an individual's access to healthcare. Students interested in public policy must recognize the interconnectedness of these factors and work towards creating comprehensive policies that address both healthcare access and social welfare.

To promote equitable healthcare access, students should engage in discussions and initiatives that aim to reduce health disparities. This may involve advocating for policies that prioritize underserved populations, promoting community health clinics, or supporting initiatives that address the social determinants of health. By understanding the complexities of healthcare access and its impact on social welfare, students can become effective advocates for change and contribute to building a more just and compassionate society.

In conclusion, healthcare access is a critical aspect of social welfare, and its impact on individuals and communities cannot be underestimated. As students interested in public policy, it is essential to explore the challenges and opportunities surrounding healthcare access and work towards creating policies that promote equity and inclusion. By understanding the role of healthcare access in social welfare, students can empower themselves to contribute to positive change in healthcare systems and advocate for a more compassionate society.

Mental Health Policies and Social Welfare

Mental Health Policies and Social Welfare: Promoting Well-being for All

In today's fast-paced and demanding world, mental health has emerged as a critical aspect of overall well-being. As students navigating through the complexities of academic life, it is essential to understand the importance of mental health policies and their relationship with social welfare. This subchapter explores the intersection of mental health, public policy, and social welfare, shedding light on the significance of addressing mental health concerns within our society.

The field of public policy plays a vital role in shaping mental health initiatives and social welfare programs. By understanding the current policies and their impact on mental health, students can actively engage in discussions and advocate for change. Mental health policies encompass a range of aspects, including access to healthcare services, funding for mental health programs, and destigmatization efforts. Exploring these policies equips students with the knowledge and tools needed to contribute to the development of effective mental health interventions.

Furthermore, social welfare systems act as a safety net for individuals experiencing mental health challenges. By examining the relationship between mental health and social welfare, students can comprehend the various support mechanisms available to individuals in need. This subchapter delves into the diverse social welfare programs, such as income support, housing assistance, and employment services, that contribute to the overall well-being of those struggling with mental health issues.

Additionally, students will explore the significance of integrating mental health policies into broader social welfare frameworks. By recognizing the interconnectedness of mental health with various social issues, such as poverty, discrimination, and inequality, students can develop a comprehensive understanding of the challenges faced by marginalized populations. This subchapter emphasizes the need for inclusive policies that address the unique mental health needs of different communities.

Through case studies, research findings, and discussions on best practices, this subchapter equips students with the knowledge and tools to engage in meaningful conversations about mental health policies and social welfare. By understanding the complexities of mental health in the context of public policy, students can become advocates for change, fostering a more compassionate and inclusive society.

In conclusion, "Mental Health Policies and Social Welfare" is a subchapter that empowers students to explore the intersection of mental health, public policy, and social welfare. By delving into the intricacies of mental health policies and their relationship with social welfare programs, students gain the knowledge and tools to actively contribute to the development of effective interventions and advocate for change. Understanding the significance of mental health within broader social welfare frameworks allows students to foster a more compassionate society that prioritizes the well-being of all individuals.

Addressing Health Disparities through Social Welfare

In the modern world, health disparities continue to persist, affecting individuals from various social and economic backgrounds. These disparities are rooted in social determinants of health, such as income, education, employment, and housing, which significantly impact an individual's well-being. As students studying public policy, it is crucial to understand the role of social welfare policies in addressing these disparities and promoting health equity for all.

Social welfare policies encompass a range of programs and initiatives designed to support individuals and communities in need. These policies aim to alleviate poverty, improve access to healthcare, and create conditions for individuals to lead healthy lives. By addressing the social determinants of health, social welfare policies play a vital role in reducing health disparities and enhancing overall well-being.

One of the key ways social welfare policies address health disparities is through the provision of affordable and accessible healthcare. Publicly funded healthcare programs, such as Medicaid and the Children's Health Insurance Program (CHIP), ensure that individuals and families with low incomes have access to necessary medical services. Additionally, social welfare policies support the creation of community health centers and clinics, which serve as primary care providers in underserved areas, bridging the healthcare gap for vulnerable populations.

Furthermore, social welfare policies focus on promoting health promotion and disease prevention. Initiatives such as nutrition assistance programs, school lunch programs, and community wellness programs aim to educate and empower individuals to make healthier choices. By addressing lifestyle factors and providing resources for healthy living, social welfare policies contribute to reducing health disparities and improving overall public health outcomes.

Another critical aspect of addressing health disparities through social welfare is the emphasis on social and economic equality. Policies that promote affordable housing, quality education, and employment opportunities contribute to creating the conditions necessary for good health. By addressing the underlying social determinants, social welfare policies work towards eliminating barriers that prevent individuals from accessing healthcare and achieving optimal health.

As students studying public policy, it is essential to recognize the interconnectedness of social welfare and health. By advocating for and shaping social welfare policies, we can contribute to creating a society where everyone has an equal opportunity to achieve good health and well-being. Through our understanding of health disparities and the power of social welfare, we can work towards a future where health equity is a reality for all.

Chapter 7: Housing and Social Welfare Policy

Affordable Housing Initiatives

In recent years, the issue of affordable housing has gained significant attention in the realm of public policy. With rising housing costs and limited availability, finding safe and affordable housing has become a pressing concern for many individuals and families. This subchapter explores the various initiatives and policies that aim to address this issue, shedding light on the importance of affordable housing for social welfare.

One of the key initiatives in the realm of affordable housing is the creation of subsidized housing programs. These programs, often led by government agencies or non-profit organizations, provide financial assistance to individuals and families who are unable to afford market-rate housing. Through subsidies and rental assistance, these programs ensure that low-income individuals have access to safe and affordable housing options.

Another approach to affordable housing is the development of mixed-income housing communities. These communities are designed to incorporate a range of housing options, including both affordable and market-rate units. By integrating individuals from different income brackets, mixed-income housing aims to foster diversity and social cohesion, while also providing affordable housing options for those in need.

Furthermore, there have been efforts to promote affordable housing through the use of tax incentives and zoning regulations.

Governments have implemented tax credits and exemptions to encourage developers to include affordable housing units in their projects. Additionally, zoning regulations can require developers to allocate a certain percentage of their developments to affordable housing, ensuring that low-income individuals have access to high-opportunity areas.

It is important for students to understand and engage with these affordable housing initiatives. By doing so, they can contribute to the ongoing dialogue about social welfare policies and advocate for change in their communities. Moreover, studying these initiatives provides students with a broader understanding of the interconnectedness of social issues and the potential impact of public policy on people's lives.

In conclusion, affordable housing initiatives play a crucial role in promoting social welfare and addressing the housing crisis. Through subsidized housing programs, mixed-income communities, tax incentives, and zoning regulations, governments and organizations are working towards ensuring that everyone has access to safe and affordable housing. As students interested in public policy, it is essential to recognize the significance of these initiatives and strive to make a positive impact in the field of affordable housing.

Homelessness and Social Welfare

In today's society, homelessness has become a pressing issue that demands our attention. As students interested in public policy, it is crucial for us to understand the complexities surrounding homelessness and the social welfare policies that aim to address this issue.

Homelessness is not simply a result of personal choices or individual failures; rather, it is a product of systemic factors such as poverty, lack of affordable housing, mental illness, and inadequate social welfare policies. Understanding these root causes is essential for developing effective strategies to combat homelessness and promote social welfare.

One of the key aspects of addressing homelessness is the role of social welfare policies. Social welfare policies are a set of governmental actions aimed at promoting the well-being of individuals and communities. These policies can range from providing emergency shelters and transitional housing to offering mental health services and employment assistance.

However, it is important to recognize that social welfare policies alone are not enough to tackle homelessness. This issue requires a comprehensive approach that combines affordable housing initiatives, supportive services, and community engagement. By adopting a holistic strategy, we can work towards long-term solutions that not only tackle homelessness but also address its underlying causes.

Furthermore, it is essential for students of public policy to critically examine existing social welfare policies and evaluate their effectiveness. By analyzing the outcomes and impacts of these policies, we can identify areas for improvement and advocate for necessary changes. This includes exploring alternative approaches such as Housing First, which prioritizes providing stable housing as a first step towards addressing homelessness.

Moreover, as students, we have the power to make a difference by engaging in advocacy and raising awareness about homelessness and social welfare policies. By collaborating with local organizations, volunteering at shelters, and participating in community initiatives, we can contribute to the ongoing efforts to combat homelessness.

In conclusion, homelessness is a complex issue that requires our attention and compassion. By understanding the root causes of homelessness and critically evaluating social welfare policies, we can work towards implementing effective strategies that promote housing stability and provide necessary support services. As students of public policy, it is our responsibility to advocate for change and contribute to creating a society that values compassion and social justice.

Housing Policies for Vulnerable Populations

In recent years, the issue of housing for vulnerable populations has become increasingly important in public policy discussions. As students interested in public policy, it is crucial for us to understand the challenges faced by these populations and the policies designed to address them.

Vulnerable populations include individuals and families who are at a higher risk of experiencing homelessness or housing instability due to various factors such as low-income, disabilities, or being victims of domestic violence. These groups often face significant barriers when trying to secure safe and affordable housing.

One key housing policy aimed at supporting vulnerable populations is the provision of affordable housing options. Affordable housing programs provide subsidies or financial assistance to low-income individuals and families, making it possible for them to access housing that they would otherwise be unable to afford. These programs are implemented at the federal, state, and local levels and are crucial in ensuring that vulnerable populations have a stable place to live.

Another important policy is supportive housing, which combines affordable housing with supportive services tailored to the needs of the population being served. Supportive housing programs target individuals experiencing chronic homelessness or those with mental health or substance abuse issues. By providing a stable home and access to necessary services, these programs help vulnerable individuals regain stability and improve their overall well-being.

Additionally, policies addressing fair housing practices are essential in protecting vulnerable populations from discrimination and ensuring equal access to housing opportunities. The Fair Housing Act prohibits discrimination based on race, color, national origin, religion, sex, familial status, and disability. It is vital for students to understand this policy and advocate for its enforcement to promote equal housing opportunities for all.

As future policymakers, it is our responsibility to be knowledgeable about these housing policies and to advocate for their improvement and expansion. By understanding the challenges faced by vulnerable populations and the policies designed to support them, we can work towards creating more inclusive and compassionate communities.

In conclusion, housing policies for vulnerable populations play a crucial role in addressing the housing needs of individuals and families at risk of homelessness or housing instability. Affordable housing options, supportive housing programs, and fair housing practices are all essential components of these policies. As students interested in public policy, it is our duty to learn about and advocate for these policies in order to create a more equitable and compassionate society for all.

Chapter 8: Employment and Social Welfare Policy

Unemployment and Job Security

In today's rapidly changing economy, the issues of unemployment and job security have emerged as critical concerns for individuals, communities, and governments across the globe. It is imperative that students, particularly those interested in public policy, gain a comprehensive understanding of these challenges and explore potential solutions.

Unemployment, simply defined as the state of being without a job, has far-reaching consequences that extend beyond financial hardships. It can lead to feelings of worthlessness, low self-esteem, and even mental health issues. For students who are about to enter the workforce, understanding the causes and effects of unemployment is crucial. Factors such as technological advancements, economic recessions, and globalization have significantly impacted the job market, often resulting in job losses and limited employment opportunities.

Job security, on the other hand, refers to the assurance that individuals have in maintaining their current employment or finding new employment if necessary. While it is an essential aspect of a stable economy, job security has become increasingly elusive in recent years. The rise of the gig economy, part-time and contract work, and the automation of various industries have all contributed to a sense of insecurity among workers.

This subchapter aims to delve deep into the complexities of unemployment and job security by examining their causes, consequences, and potential policy solutions. By providing a comprehensive overview, students will be able to grasp the multifaceted nature of the issue and develop informed opinions on how to address it.

Furthermore, this subchapter will explore the role of social welfare policies in mitigating the adverse effects of unemployment and ensuring job security for individuals. It will delve into topics such as unemployment benefits, retraining programs, and labor market regulations. By analyzing these policies, students will gain insight into the ways governments and societies can support individuals during periods of unemployment and foster job security in the long run.

Ultimately, this subchapter aims to equip students with the knowledge and tools necessary to navigate the complex landscape of unemployment and job security. By understanding the underlying causes, consequences, and potential solutions, students can actively contribute to the development and implementation of effective social welfare policies that promote a more inclusive and equitable society.

Minimum Wage and Income Support

Minimum Wage and Income Support

Introduction:

In this subchapter, we will delve into the crucial topic of minimum wage and income support. As students interested in public policy, it is essential to understand the nuances of these policies, which have a direct impact on individuals and families facing economic challenges. We will explore the rationale behind minimum wage laws, their effects on employment and poverty rates, as well as income support programs designed to alleviate financial hardships. By gaining a comprehensive understanding of these policies, we can contribute to informed discussions and shape the future of social welfare.

Minimum Wage Laws:

Minimum wage laws aim to establish a floor for wages, ensuring that workers receive a fair and decent income. By examining the historical context and economic implications, we can better understand the reasons behind minimum wage legislation. We will explore how these laws protect vulnerable workers from exploitation and contribute to reducing income inequality. Additionally, we will analyze the potential drawbacks, such as potential job losses and impacts on small businesses, to present a balanced perspective.

Effects on Employment and Poverty Rates:

One of the key debates surrounding minimum wage laws revolves around their impact on employment rates. We will critically analyze empirical studies to determine whether raising the minimum wage leads to job losses or stimulates economic growth. Furthermore, we will examine the effects of minimum wage on poverty rates and discuss its role in reducing income disparities.

Income Support Programs:

Income support programs play a vital role in assisting individuals and families who face financial challenges. We will explore various forms of income support, such as welfare, food stamps, and housing assistance. By understanding the eligibility criteria, benefits, and limitations of these programs, we can evaluate their effectiveness in reducing poverty and promoting social mobility.

Reforms and Future Directions:

As students interested in public policy, it is crucial to be aware of ongoing debates, proposed reforms, and innovative approaches to minimum wage and income support policies. We will explore potential reforms, such as increasing the minimum wage to a living wage and expanding income support programs. Additionally, we will discuss the importance of evidence-based policymaking and the role of advocacy in shaping social welfare policies.

Conclusion:

Understanding the intricacies of minimum wage and income support policies is crucial for students interested in public policy. By examining the rationale, effects, and potential reforms of these policies, we can contribute to informed discussions, advocate for evidence-based approaches, and ultimately work towards a more compassionate and equitable society.

Workforce Development Programs for Students

In today's fast-paced and competitive job market, it is essential for students to equip themselves with the necessary skills and knowledge to thrive in their chosen careers. Workforce development programs offer unique opportunities for students to gain valuable experience and enhance their employability. In this subchapter, we will explore the various workforce development programs available to students and the significant impact they can have on their future.

Workforce development programs are designed to bridge the gap between education and employment by providing students with practical training, internships, and mentorship opportunities. These programs are often offered by government agencies, non-profit organizations, and private companies, with a focus on developing a highly skilled and adaptable workforce. By participating in these programs, students can gain real-world experience, network with professionals, and develop essential skills that will make them stand out in the job market.

One prominent example of a workforce development program is apprenticeships. Apprenticeships provide students with the opportunity to learn a trade or profession through a combination of on-the-job training and classroom instruction. This hands-on approach allows students to acquire practical skills under the guidance of experienced mentors. Apprenticeships are particularly beneficial for students interested in skilled trades, such as carpentry, plumbing, or electrician work, as they provide a direct pathway to a rewarding and well-paid career.

Another valuable workforce development program is internships. Internships enable students to gain valuable work experience in their field of interest while still in school. Whether paid or unpaid, internships provide students with the chance to apply their knowledge in a real-world setting, learn from professionals, and build a network of contacts. Internships are instrumental in helping students explore different career paths, gain industry-specific skills, and make informed decisions about their future.

Furthermore, mentorship programs play a crucial role in workforce development. These programs pair students with experienced professionals who can guide and advise them on their career journey. Mentors provide valuable insights, share industry knowledge, and offer support and encouragement to help students succeed. Through mentorship programs, students can develop essential soft skills, receive career guidance, and build a strong professional network.

In conclusion, workforce development programs offer students a valuable platform to gain practical skills, explore career opportunities, and enhance their employability. By participating in apprenticeships, internships, and mentorship programs, students can gain a competitive edge in the job market and set themselves up for success in their chosen fields. It is essential for students interested in public policy to actively seek out these programs and take advantage of the unique opportunities they provide. By doing so, they can pave the way for a promising and fulfilling career in public policy.

Chapter 9: Social Welfare Policy and Social Justice Movements

Intersectionality and Social Welfare

In recent years, the concept of intersectionality has gained significant attention in the field of social welfare and public policy. Intersectionality refers to the interconnected nature of social categorizations such as race, gender, class, and other identities, as they create overlapping and interdependent systems of discrimination and disadvantage. Understanding intersectionality is crucial in developing effective social welfare policies that address the diverse needs and experiences of individuals and communities.

In the context of social welfare, intersectionality recognizes that individuals may face multiple forms of oppression and discrimination simultaneously. For example, a person who identifies as a woman may face gender-based discrimination, but she may also experience racism if she belongs to a racial minority. These intersecting identities can compound the challenges faced by individuals, making it essential for policymakers to consider the unique circumstances of different groups.

Recognizing intersectionality in social welfare policy is vital for achieving equitable outcomes. Traditional approaches to social welfare often overlook the unique experiences of marginalized groups, leading to policies that fail to address their specific needs. By adopting an intersectional lens, policymakers can develop more inclusive and effective policies that consider the diverse experiences and needs of all individuals.

One example of the intersectionality approach in social welfare is the development of targeted programs for marginalized communities. Rather than implementing a one-size-fits-all approach, policymakers can design initiatives that take into account the specific challenges faced by different groups. For instance, a social welfare program aimed at reducing homelessness may need to address not only the lack of affordable housing but also the racial disparities that contribute to higher rates of homelessness among certain communities.

Intersectionality also emphasizes the importance of involving diverse voices in policy development. By including individuals from different backgrounds and experiences, policymakers can gain insights into the unique challenges faced by marginalized groups and develop more comprehensive and effective solutions.

In conclusion, understanding intersectionality is crucial in the field of social welfare and public policy. By recognizing the interconnected nature of social categorizations and the resulting systems of discrimination, policymakers can develop inclusive and effective policies that address the diverse needs and experiences of individuals and communities. Integrating an intersectional perspective into social welfare policy can lead to more equitable outcomes and ensure that no one is left behind.

LGBTQ+ Rights and Social Welfare

In recent years, there has been a remarkable shift in public opinion regarding LGBTQ+ rights, and it is important for students interested in public policy to understand the intersection of these rights with social welfare. The LGBTQ+ community has long faced discrimination, marginalization, and unequal treatment, making it a crucial topic within the realm of social welfare policy.

One of the fundamental principles of social welfare is the promotion of equality and justice for all individuals, regardless of their sexual orientation or gender identity. LGBTQ+ rights encompass a wide range of issues, including marriage equality, adoption rights, employment protections, and access to healthcare. These rights directly impact the well-being and overall quality of life of LGBTQ+ individuals, making it essential to examine the policies in place to address these concerns.

Historically, the LGBTQ+ community has been disproportionately affected by social welfare issues such as homelessness, mental health disparities, and substance abuse due to the discrimination they face. Therefore, it is crucial for students studying public policy to understand the specific challenges faced by this community and to advocate for inclusive policies that address these disparities.

For instance, implementing comprehensive anti-discrimination laws that protect LGBTQ+ individuals in employment, housing, and public accommodations is an essential step towards ensuring equal opportunities for all. Students should also explore policies that promote safe and inclusive schools, as LGBTQ+ youth are more likely to face bullying and harassment, leading to lower academic achievement and increased rates of mental health issues.

Moreover, healthcare policies should be examined from an LGBTQ+ perspective. LGBTQ+ individuals often face barriers to accessing gender-affirming healthcare, mental health services, and HIV prevention and treatment. Students interested in public policy can explore policies that address these disparities, such as expanding Medicaid coverage for transgender healthcare or supporting initiatives that provide culturally competent healthcare services for LGBTQ+ individuals.

By recognizing the importance of LGBTQ+ rights within the realm of social welfare policy, students can contribute to creating a more inclusive society. This subchapter provides an overview of the challenges faced by the LGBTQ+ community and highlights the policies and initiatives that address these issues. By understanding the intersectionality of LGBTQ+ rights and social welfare, students can actively engage in shaping policies that promote equality, justice, and compassion for all individuals, regardless of their sexual orientation or gender identity.

Racial Justice and Social Welfare

In this subchapter, we will delve into the crucial intersection of racial justice and social welfare, shedding light on the challenges faced by marginalized communities and exploring policies aimed at fostering equality and inclusivity. By understanding the importance of racial justice in public policy, students can contribute to creating a fairer and more compassionate society.

Racial disparities persist in various areas of social welfare, including education, healthcare, housing, and criminal justice. These inequities are deeply rooted in historical and systemic racism, perpetuating cycles of poverty and exclusion. As students studying public policy, it is essential to recognize these injustices and work towards dismantling the structures that perpetuate them.

One major aspect of racial justice in social welfare is education. Students from marginalized communities often face unequal access to quality education, limited resources, and discriminatory practices. Addressing these disparities requires comprehensive policies that focus on equitable funding, culturally sensitive curriculum, and support systems for students facing socio-economic challenges.

Another critical area to explore is healthcare. Racial and ethnic minorities often experience disparities in access to healthcare services, leading to poorer health outcomes. Public policy initiatives must strive to eliminate these disparities by ensuring affordable and accessible healthcare for all, promoting diversity in the healthcare workforce, and addressing implicit biases within the system.

Housing is another key aspect where racial justice intersects with social welfare. Historically, marginalized communities have been subjected to discriminatory housing practices, such as redlining and gentrification. Policies must aim to provide affordable housing options, combat housing discrimination, and promote inclusive communities.

Additionally, the criminal justice system disproportionately affects communities of color. Policies that address racial profiling, sentencing disparities, and the overrepresentation of minorities in prisons are crucial to promote racial justice and social welfare.

To create a society that upholds racial justice in social welfare, it is vital for students to engage in advocacy and activism. By raising awareness, participating in protests, and supporting organizations fighting for equality, students can contribute to meaningful change.

By exploring racial justice in social welfare, students studying public policy can gain the knowledge and skills necessary to advocate for equitable policies that address the needs of marginalized communities. Together, we can build a society where everyone has equal access to opportunities, resources, and social support, creating a more compassionate and just world for all.

Chapter 10: Ethical Considerations in Social Welfare Policy

Ethics and Decision-Making in Social Welfare

In the field of social welfare, the decisions made by policymakers have a profound impact on individuals and communities. As students of public policy, it is crucial for us to understand the ethical considerations and decision-making processes that underpin social welfare policies. This subchapter explores the complex relationship between ethics and decision-making in social welfare, shedding light on the moral dilemmas faced by policymakers and the potential consequences of their choices.

Ethics form the foundation of social welfare policy, guiding policymakers in their pursuit of a just and compassionate society. It involves the examination of values, principles, and moral norms that shape our understanding of right and wrong. When making decisions, policymakers must consider the ethical implications of their choices, ensuring that their actions align with ethical standards and promote the well-being of the individuals they seek to serve.

One of the key ethical challenges in social welfare decision-making is striking a balance between individual rights and collective responsibility. Policymakers must grapple with the tension between upholding individual autonomy and ensuring equitable distribution of resources. For instance, in allocating limited funds for welfare programs, policymakers must decide who should receive assistance and to what extent, while also considering the potential consequences of their decisions on the larger society.

Moreover, ethical decision-making in social welfare requires a consideration of social justice principles. Policies must aim to reduce inequalities and address systemic injustices that perpetuate poverty and marginalization. By understanding the root causes of social inequalities, policymakers can develop interventions that promote fairness and equal opportunities for all members of society.

Transparency and accountability are also essential components of ethical decision-making in social welfare. Policymakers must be transparent in their decision-making processes, ensuring that their choices are guided by objective evidence and public input. They must be accountable for the consequences of their decisions, regularly evaluating the impact of social welfare policies and making necessary adjustments to address any unintended negative outcomes.

As future policymakers, it is imperative for students of public policy to critically engage with the ethical dimensions of social welfare decision-making. By examining the ethical principles that underpin social welfare policies, we can better understand the challenges faced by policymakers and contribute to the development of more just and compassionate social welfare systems. Through our commitment to ethical decision-making, we can harness the power of compassion to create positive change in society.

Balancing Individual Rights and Collective Well-being

In today's society, the concept of balancing individual rights and collective well-being has become increasingly important. As students interested in public policy, it is crucial to understand the delicate balance between personal freedoms and the greater good of society. In this subchapter, we will explore the complexities of this issue and the potential implications for social welfare policy.

Individual rights are the fundamental liberties and freedoms that every person is entitled to, such as freedom of speech, religion, and privacy. These rights form the cornerstone of a democratic society, empowering individuals to express themselves and pursue their own goals. However, it is essential to recognize that these rights are not absolute and can sometimes conflict with the well-being of the community.

Collective well-being refers to the overall welfare and happiness of society as a whole, taking into account the needs and interests of the entire population. This includes ensuring access to education, healthcare, and social support systems, among others. Social welfare policies are designed to promote the collective well-being by providing a safety net for those in need and addressing systemic inequalities.

One of the key challenges in balancing individual rights and collective well-being lies in finding the right balance between personal freedoms and societal obligations. For example, while freedom of speech is crucial, it must be balanced with the responsibility to avoid hate speech or incitement to violence that could harm the well-being of others. Similarly, the right to privacy must be weighed against the need for transparency in government and security concerns.

Moreover, there are instances where individual rights may need to be constrained for the greater good. For instance, during public health emergencies, temporary limitations on individual freedoms may be necessary to protect public health. These decisions often involve difficult trade-offs and require careful consideration of the potential impact on both individuals and society.

As students of public policy, it is our responsibility to critically analyze the ethical and practical implications of balancing individual rights and collective well-being. By studying various case studies and engaging in thoughtful discussions, we can gain a deeper understanding of the complexities involved in policymaking. This knowledge will equip us with the necessary tools to navigate the challenges of creating effective social welfare policies that prioritize both individual rights and the collective well-being of our society.

In conclusion, the subchapter "Balancing Individual Rights and Collective Well-being" explores the intricate relationship between personal freedoms and the welfare of society as a whole. As students interested in public policy, it is crucial for us to understand the complexities of this issue and the potential implications for social welfare policy. By examining different perspectives and engaging in thoughtful discussions, we can contribute to the development of policies that protect individual rights while promoting the collective well-being of our communities.

Ethical Dilemmas in Social Welfare Policy

In the realm of public policy, social welfare policies play a crucial role in addressing societal issues and promoting the well-being of individuals and communities. However, these policies are often accompanied by ethical dilemmas that policymakers and students in the field of public policy must grapple with. Understanding and navigating these ethical dilemmas is essential for creating effective and compassionate social welfare policies.

One prominent ethical dilemma in social welfare policy is the tension between individual rights and societal responsibility. On one hand, individuals have the right to personal autonomy and privacy, and social welfare policies should respect and protect these rights. However, societal responsibility requires the allocation of resources and intervention to address social problems. Balancing individual rights with the greater good of society is a complex ethical challenge that policymakers and students must confront.

Another ethical dilemma arises from the limited resources available for social welfare programs. In the face of budget constraints, policymakers must make difficult decisions about how to allocate resources to different social welfare initiatives. This necessitates prioritizing certain groups or issues over others, potentially leaving some individuals without the assistance they need. Students studying public policy must grapple with questions of fairness and equity in resource allocation, ensuring that the most vulnerable populations are not left behind.

Furthermore, social welfare policies can sometimes perpetuate dependency or stigmatize individuals who rely on them. While these policies are intended to provide support, they can inadvertently create cycles of dependency or reinforce negative stereotypes about recipients. Policymakers and students must navigate the fine line between providing necessary assistance and empowering individuals to become self-sufficient.

Lastly, cultural and moral values can also pose ethical dilemmas in social welfare policy. Different societies and communities hold diverse beliefs and norms, making it challenging to develop policies that satisfy everyone's ethical standards. Students must consider cultural sensitivity and inclusivity when designing social welfare policies, ensuring that they respect diverse perspectives while promoting social justice.

Understanding and addressing these ethical dilemmas is essential for creating effective and compassionate social welfare policies. By grappling with the tension between individual rights and societal responsibility, making equitable resource allocations, empowering individuals, and respecting cultural diversity, students studying public policy can contribute to the development of ethical and impactful social welfare policies that promote the power of compassion.

Chapter 11: Future Directions of Social Welfare Policy

Emerging Issues in Social Welfare

In today's rapidly changing world, social welfare policies play a crucial role in addressing the needs of individuals and communities. As students pursuing a career in public policy, it is essential to stay up-to-date with the emerging issues in social welfare. This subchapter aims to provide an overview of some key challenges and concerns that are shaping the social welfare landscape.

1. Inequality and Poverty: One of the most pressing issues in social welfare is the widening gap between the rich and the poor. Income inequality and persistent poverty continue to affect millions of individuals worldwide. As students, it is crucial to understand the root causes of inequality and poverty and explore innovative approaches to address these issues.

2. Aging Population: With advancements in healthcare and increased life expectancy, the global population is aging rapidly. This demographic shift poses unique challenges for social welfare systems, including healthcare, retirement, and long-term care services. As policymakers, it is important to develop strategies that promote active aging and ensure the well-being of older adults.

3. Mental Health: Mental health has gained significant attention in recent years, highlighting the need for improved access to mental health services. Students must familiarize themselves with the current mental health landscape, including the prevalence of mental health

disorders, the impact of stigma, and the importance of early intervention and prevention.

4. Climate Change and Environmental Justice: The increasing frequency and intensity of natural disasters have brought attention to the intersection between social welfare and the environment. Climate change disproportionately affects vulnerable populations, exacerbating existing inequalities. Understanding the concept of environmental justice and its implications for social welfare policies is crucial for future policymakers.

5. Technology and Automation: The rapid advancement of technology, including automation and artificial intelligence, has the potential to reshape the job market and create new challenges for social welfare. As students, it is important to explore the impact of technology on employment, income distribution, and social protection, as well as potential policy responses.

By familiarizing ourselves with these emerging issues in social welfare, we can become better equipped to advocate for effective policies that promote social justice and improve the well-being of individuals and communities. The field of social welfare is dynamic and constantly evolving, and as students in public policy, it is our duty to stay informed, engage in critical discussions, and work towards creating a more compassionate and equitable society.

Innovative Approaches to Social Welfare Policy

As students interested in the field of public policy, it is crucial to explore innovative approaches to social welfare policy that have the potential to create positive and lasting change in society. In this subchapter, we will delve into some of the most cutting-edge strategies and ideas that are currently shaping the field of social welfare policy.

One innovative approach that has gained significant attention in recent years is the concept of universal basic income (UBI). UBI is a policy that guarantees a certain income level to all individuals, regardless of their employment status. Proponents argue that UBI can alleviate poverty, reduce inequality, and provide individuals with the freedom to pursue their passions and aspirations. By exploring the successes and challenges of UBI pilot programs around the world, students can gain a deeper understanding of the potential of this approach in addressing social welfare issues.

Another innovative approach to social welfare policy is the implementation of social impact bonds (SIBs). SIBs are a unique financing mechanism that brings together private investors, social service providers, and government agencies to address social issues. By utilizing a pay-for-success model, SIBs incentivize the achievement of specific social outcomes, such as reducing homelessness or improving educational attainment. This approach encourages collaboration between sectors and shifts the focus from inputs to measurable outcomes, thereby increasing accountability and efficiency in social welfare programs.

Furthermore, the use of technology and data analytics has revolutionized the field of social welfare policy. With the advent of big data and machine learning, policymakers can now analyze vast amounts of information to identify trends, predict outcomes, and allocate resources more effectively. For example, predictive analytics can be utilized to identify individuals at risk of homelessness or child abuse, enabling early intervention and prevention strategies. By understanding the potential of technology in social welfare policy, students can explore how data-driven approaches can lead to more targeted and efficient interventions.

In conclusion, innovative approaches to social welfare policy are essential for addressing the complex challenges of our time. By delving into concepts such as universal basic income, social impact bonds, and the use of technology and data analytics, students can gain a comprehensive understanding of the evolving landscape of social welfare policy. As future policymakers, it is crucial to explore these innovative approaches and consider their potential impact on creating a more compassionate and just society.

Students' Role in Shaping the Future of Social Welfare Policy

As students, you have the power to shape the future of social welfare policy. Your energy, ideas, and passion can make a significant impact on the lives of individuals and communities who are in need. This subchapter will explore how students can play a crucial role in influencing public policy and creating a more compassionate society.

One way students can contribute to the development of social welfare policy is through research and analysis. By conducting in-depth research on social issues and their underlying causes, you can provide valuable insights and evidence that policymakers can use to make informed decisions. Whether it is studying the impact of poverty on education or the effectiveness of healthcare programs, your research can help shape policies that address these issues more effectively.

Furthermore, students can engage in advocacy and activism to raise awareness and promote change. By organizing rallies, writing letters to policymakers, or using social media platforms to spread the word, you can bring attention to the pressing issues that require immediate action. Your voices and actions can create a groundswell of support, encouraging policymakers to prioritize social welfare policies and make them a top priority.

Another way students can contribute is by participating in internships and volunteering opportunities. By getting involved in organizations and agencies that work on social welfare issues, you can gain firsthand experience and insight into the challenges faced by marginalized populations. This direct exposure will enable you to offer valuable perspectives and recommendations when it comes to shaping policies that address these challenges effectively.

Furthermore, students can engage in dialogue and collaboration with policymakers and stakeholders. By attending public hearings, town hall meetings, or joining policy-focused organizations, you can directly contribute to the policy-making process. Your input, ideas, and suggestions will be valuable in shaping policies that are inclusive, equitable, and centered around the needs of the most vulnerable in society.

Lastly, students can engage in educational efforts by spreading awareness and knowledge about social welfare policies. By organizing workshops, seminars, or guest lectures, you can educate your peers and community about the importance of social welfare policies and the impact they have on individuals and society as a whole. By empowering others with knowledge, you can inspire them to also take action and create positive change.

In conclusion, as students interested in public policy, you have a critical role to play in shaping the future of social welfare policy. Through research, advocacy, volunteer work, collaboration, and education, you can make a lasting impact on the lives of those in need. By harnessing your passion and dedication, you can contribute to the creation of a more compassionate society, where no one is left behind.

Chapter 12: Conclusion

Recap of Key Learnings

As students exploring the fascinating realm of social welfare policy, we have delved into the depths of understanding the power of compassion and its impact on society. Throughout our journey in this book, "The Power of Compassion: Exploring Social Welfare Policy for Students," we have gained valuable insights into the intricacies of public policy and its role in shaping the lives of individuals and communities.

One of the key learnings we have acquired is the significance of empathy in the development and implementation of social welfare policies. We have come to understand that compassionate policies not only alleviate the suffering of the marginalized but also foster a sense of collective responsibility and solidarity within society. By considering the needs and experiences of the most vulnerable, we can create a more just and equitable society.

Additionally, our exploration of public policy has revealed the importance of evidence-based decision-making. We have learned that policies driven by rigorous research and data analysis are more likely to yield positive outcomes. This knowledge empowers us as students to advocate for evidence-based policy solutions and to critically evaluate the effectiveness of existing policies.

Moreover, we have discovered that social welfare policies are not static but evolve in response to societal changes and emerging challenges. By examining historical policy developments, we have gained a deeper understanding of the factors that shape policy agendas and how policies can be adapted to meet the needs of an ever-changing world.

Furthermore, our journey has highlighted the significance of collaboration and interdisciplinary approaches in addressing complex social issues. We have explored the interconnectedness of various fields, such as healthcare, education, and housing, and how policies in these domains intersect to create comprehensive solutions.

Lastly, our exploration of social welfare policy has emphasized the importance of active citizenship and engagement. As students, we now comprehend the power of our voices and the role we can play in advocating for policy changes. By being informed, critical, and active participants in the policy-making process, we can strive towards a society that upholds compassion and social justice.

In conclusion, "The Power of Compassion: Exploring Social Welfare Policy for Students" has provided us with a comprehensive understanding of the intricate world of public policy. Through empathy, evidence-based decision-making, adaptability, collaboration, and active citizenship, we can harness the power of compassion to create a more equitable and compassionate society. As students, we have the potential to become change agents and shape the future of social welfare policy for the betterment of all.

Empowering Students to Advocate for Social Welfare Policy

As students, you possess a unique power to effect change in society. Your passion, energy, and idealism can transform the world around you. One area where you can make a significant impact is in advocating for social welfare policy. This subchapter aims to equip you with the knowledge and tools necessary to become effective advocates for change.

Understanding the importance of social welfare policy is crucial. It encompasses a wide range of issues such as healthcare, education, housing, and poverty alleviation. By advocating for policies that promote social justice and equality, you can help create a more inclusive and compassionate society.

The first step in becoming an advocate is to educate yourself about the issues. Research and analyze existing policies, identify their strengths and weaknesses, and understand the impact they have on different communities. Stay updated on current events and news related to social welfare policy, as this will provide you with a better understanding of the challenges faced by various marginalized groups.

Once you have a solid understanding of the issues, it's time to take action. Start by joining student organizations or clubs that focus on public policy and social justice. These groups provide a platform for like-minded individuals to come together, share ideas, and collaborate on advocacy initiatives.

Develop your advocacy skills by attending workshops, conferences, and seminars. These events offer valuable insights into effective communication, policy analysis, and grassroots organizing.

Additionally, they provide opportunities to network with professionals and activists in the field, allowing you to learn from their experiences and gain mentorship.

Utilize the power of social media to raise awareness about social welfare issues. Create engaging content, share informative articles, and mobilize your peers to support your cause. By leveraging the reach of social media platforms, you can amplify your voice and reach a wider audience.

Another crucial aspect of advocacy is engaging with policymakers. Write letters or emails to your local representatives, expressing your concerns and recommendations for policy reform. Attend town hall meetings or public hearings to voice your opinions and share personal stories that highlight the importance of social welfare policy.

Remember, change takes time and perseverance. Be patient and resilient in your advocacy efforts. Celebrate small victories and learn from setbacks. By empowering yourself and others to advocate for social welfare policy, you can contribute to building a more just and compassionate society for all.

Final Thoughts on the Power of Compassion

Compassion has always been at the heart of effective social welfare policies. Throughout this book, we have explored various aspects of social welfare policies and how they impact individuals and communities. As students, it is crucial for us to grasp the power of compassion and its role in shaping public policy.

Compassion is not just a mere emotion; it is a driving force that has the potential to create significant positive change. When we approach policy-making with compassion, we are guided by empathy and a genuine desire to improve the lives of those who are marginalized or disadvantaged. It is through compassion that we can recognize the inherent worth and dignity of every individual, regardless of their circumstances.

As students studying public policy, we have a unique opportunity to understand and shape the social welfare policies that govern our society. By embracing compassion, we can challenge the existing systems and advocate for policies that prioritize the well-being of all individuals, especially those who are most vulnerable.

Compassion allows us to see beyond statistics and data, to truly understand the lived experiences of those affected by these policies. It fuels our determination to alleviate suffering and create a more just and equitable society. By incorporating compassion into our policy-making process, we can ensure that the voices and needs of the marginalized are heard and addressed.

However, it is important to acknowledge that compassion alone is not enough. To bring about lasting change, we must also combine it with knowledge, research, and evidence-based practices. By integrating compassion with rigorous analysis, we can formulate policies that are not only well-intentioned but also effective in improving social welfare outcomes.

As students, we must also recognize the power and privilege that comes with our education. We have a responsibility to use this privilege to advocate for those who have been silenced or overlooked. By harnessing the power of compassion, we can become catalysts for change and contribute to a more compassionate and inclusive society.

In conclusion, the power of compassion cannot be understated when it comes to shaping social welfare policies. As students of public policy, we have the opportunity to embrace compassion as a guiding principle and drive positive change in our society. By combining empathy with rigorous analysis, we can create policies that prioritize the well-being and dignity of all individuals. Let us harness the power of compassion and work towards a more just and compassionate world.

www.ingramcontent.com/pod-product-compliance
Lightning Source LLC
LaVergne TN
LVHW051310200726
843510LV00010B/1346